SPECTACULAR
CANADA

SPECTACULAR
CANADA

Elaine Jones

SMITHBOOKS

Smithbooks
113 Merton Street
Toronto, Ontario
M4S 1A8

Edited by Linda Ostrowalker
Cover and interior design by Carolyn Deby
Front cover photograph by Dale Wilson/First Light
Back cover photograph by Alan Marsh/First Light
Typography by CompuType, Vancouver, B.C.
Printed and bound in Canada by D.W. Friesen and Sons Ltd., Altona, Manitoba

Canadian Cataloguing in Publication Data

Jones, Elaine
    Spectacular Canada

    ISBN 1-55110-050-9

    1. Canada—Pictorial works. I. Title
FC59.J66 1993   717.064'7'0222   C93-091152-0   F1017.J66 1993

Contents

. . .

Introduction

How does one take the measure of a country like Canada? Facts and figures can tell part of the story. Canada is a huge country, the second-largest in the world after Russia, covering an area of almost 10 million square kilometres. Characterized as a northern country, its territory extends beyond the Arctic Circle. Its population of more than 27,296,000 people is concentrated in its southern regions and thinly spread over its vast northern reaches. Bordered on three sides by oceans—the Atlantic, Pacific, and Arctic—its boundary to the south with the United States has been called the "longest undefended border in the world."

A typical prairie scene—grain elevators at Shaunovan, Saskatchewan.

The Canadian landscape is enormously diverse. Several mountain ranges give the land its rugged character: the older, more gentle Laurentians in the east, the famous Rockies that rise so dramatically from the wide expanse of the prairies, and the other ranges of the Western Cordillera that extend west to the Pacific coast. Mid-country, the prairies stretch for 1,500 kilometres from Manitoba to Alberta, a checkerboard landscape of small towns, farmhouses, and fields. Canada is not just a large land, it is a land of abundant water. A glance at a map shows the myriad lakes that cover the north. Powerful rivers—the St. Lawrence, Churchill, and Fraser, for example—helped open the country to exploration and are part of essential transportation and power networks today. Every Canadian schoolchild learns about the Canadian Shield: composed of the oldest rock on earth, it covers much of the eastern provinces and has become part of the collective Canadian identity.

And there are the resources provided by this diverse land: its fishery, forests, minerals, hydroelectric power, and agricultural products. Canada is the world's fifth-largest producer of wheat, the largest supplier of zinc, and the leading exporter of manufactured forest products. Not least is the considerable resource of Canada's natural beauty. Visitors enjoy the splendour of Niagara Falls and traditional beauty spots such as Lake Louise in Banff National Park, the pastoral charm of the maritime provinces and other rural areas, the opportunity of skiing some of the world's best slopes in the Rockies, and fly-in trips to virtually untouched northern wilderness where few have been before. Diverse habitat allows a wide range of life-forms, and the variety and abundance of Canada's wildlife is known around the world. While the traditional occupations of hunting, fishing, and trapping are still important, a growing number of people are enjoying a different type of wilderness experience—instead of capturing animals, they use binoculars or a camera lens to admire them in their natural habitat.

Its human resources are perhaps Canada's greatest strength: many international strands have joined together to form a country whose population is as diverse as its landscape. To its First Nations peoples were added the two main streams of modern Canada, the English and French. Immigrants from around the world came over the next few centuries, creating the rich cultural mosaic that is a characteristic of Canadian society. Communities range from the historic neighbourhoods of Quebec City and the nation's capital, Ottawa, to the sophistication of Montreal and Toronto, the friendliness of smaller cities and towns, and the vigour of younger communities in the north.

Opposite: Nova Scotia's Cape Breton Highlands National Park displays brilliant fall colour.

Newfoundland and Labrador

Newfoundland, perhaps the first part of North America explored by visitors from Europe, was the last province to join Confederation, in 1949. Viking sailors probably first set foot on Newfoundland soil in the tenth century. Five hundred years later, the Grand Banks, teeming with cod and other riches of the Atlantic, attracted Basque, French, and Portuguese fishermen. John Cabot "discovered" the island for England's King Henry VII in 1497, and by the late sixteenth century there were already settlements along the coast. Yet Newfoundland, isolated from the continent by the stormy Gulf of St. Lawrence, has developed a culture and identity unique in Canada.

The rich fishery that first attracted explorers has been the main staple of Newfoundland's economy ever since. Outports—tiny villages accessible only by boat—grew up along the many bays and fiords of the deeply indented shores. Isolation and the rigours of the North Atlantic fostered a fierce independence among villagers and allowed the preservation of dialects found nowhere else in Canada.

The capital and largest city of Newfoundland is St. John's, with a population of about 172,000—almost one-third of the province's total. It is located on the Avalon Peninsula, the first part of Newfoundland settled by Europeans, and once the main centre for the fishing industry. St. John's later became a supply centre for Atlantic fishing fleets, and the discovery of major offshore oil deposits has given the city new life. Built on bluffs surrounding a deep harbour, its distinctive multicoloured wooden houses rise in tiers. Its narrow streets and turn-

The capital of Newfoundland, St. John's is noted for its colourful wooden buildings along the waterfront.

of-the-century buildings preserve the historic core of the city, while modern buildings represent a renewed hope in the future of the province. Guarding the entrance to the harbour is Signal Hill. Fortifications in the national historic park recall the struggle between French and English for the new territory. Near Cabot Tower, built in 1897 to commemorate the 400th anniversary of the discovery of Newfoundland, Guglielmo Marconi received the first transatlantic wireless message in 1901.

The island of Newfoundland is one of two separate areas that form the province of Newfoundland. The mainland territory of Labrador is much larger than the island, but there are few permanent settlements. The land is forbidding—barren rock and tundra with a deeply forested interior—and the climate, subject to the frigid Labrador Current that chokes the coast with ice for six months of the year, is daunting. Underlaid with the mineral-rich rock of the Canadian Shield, Labrador also has great potential for development of hydroelectric resources.

Newfoundland's rugged beauty, once appreciated mainly by its residents, is now a draw for visitors who fly in or make the six-hour ferry crossing to Port au Basques or the twelve-hour trip to Argentia. Terra Nova and Gros Morne national parks on the east and west coasts of the island preserve some of Newfoundland's most spectacular scenic areas. Because the mainland and the interior of the island are largely uninhabited, it provides good habitat for a variety of wildlife, and large animals, such as caribou, moose, black bear, and polar bear on the mainland, are frequently spotted.

Opposite: Mist surrounds a dock at Rose Blanche, Newfoundland.

Above: Cape St. Mary's, on the Avalon Peninsula, is the site of a provincial seabird sanctuary.

Opposite: Bonavista, on Newfoundland's northeast coast, is one of the oldest communities in North America and is still an important fishing centre.

Above: Labrador's Torngat Mountains are a rugged wilderness, where vegetation is sparse and the landscape dramatic.

Opposite: Lobster pots at Fox Harbour, one of many small coves and ports that ring Placentia Bay.

Above: The provincial Legislature Building in St. John's.

Opposite: Cabot Tower, in Signal Hill National Park, was built in 1897 to commemorate the four-hundredth anniversary of John Cabot's voyage.

Above: Sunset tints the snow-clad hills at Nain, the most northerly community on the Labrador coast.

Opposite: A boat and boathouse show signs of many years of hard use at Mortier, near the fishing centre of Burin.

The Maritimes

Collectively known as the Maritimes, New Brunswick, Nova Scotia, and Prince Edward Island have an important element in common—their position on the Atlantic seaboard. While each is dominated by the sea to some extent, the country's three smallest provinces are distinctly individual.

New Brunswick is most closely connected to the mainland, bordered to the north with Quebec and to the west with Maine in the United States. Its development has been influenced by these neighbours: an influx of Loyalists during the American Revolution helped New Brunswick attain separate colonial status from Nova Scotia, and French Acadians were among the first European settlers. The expulsion of the Acadians and their later repatriation is a poignant chapter in the province's history, and today New Brunswick is Canada's only officially bilingual province. New Brunswick is heavily forested and forest industries have played a primary role in the economic life of the province, along with agriculture, mining, and the fishery. The capital, Fredericton, is on the picturesque St. John River, which has been harnessed for hydroelectric power but remains one of Canada's most scenic waterways.

Nova Scotia, connected to the mainland by the narrow Isthmus of Chignecto, is permeated with the ambience of the sea. No part of Nova Scotia is more than 56 kilometres from salt water. Fishing and related industries are central to this province, attested to by the many small villages in harbours along the deeply indented shoreline. Their charm is not lost on tourists, who flock to places like Peggy's Cove on the south shore. The Cabot

Peggy's Cove, picturesque in all its moods, is probably Nova Scotia's best-known fishing village.

Trail on Cape Breton Island has also become known as one of the world's finest scenic tours. The route skirts the spectacular headlands of the cape, daring 300-metre sheer drops to the sea and providing panoramic views of rocky shores and the highlands. The capital and largest city in Nova Scotia is Halifax, with a population of 320,000. Its historic importance is recalled in many heritage buildings and sites, such as the star-shaped Citadel. Built between 1828 and 1856 on the site of three previous forts and used as a military base into the twentieth century, it was declared a national historic park in 1956.

Canada's smallest province, Prince Edward Island is just 224 kilometres long and 6 to 64 kilometres wide. Most of the province is under cultivation, and it is perhaps best known for its rich red soil, which produces abundant potato crops. Prince Edward Island has Canada's highest concentration of population, but it retains a rural character: Charlottetown, the provincial capital, is its only incorporated city, with about 16,000 of the island's total of 130,000 people. A pretty centre with its tree-lined streets and gracious homes, Charlottetown is considered to be the birthplace of Canadian Confederation; although Prince Edward Island did not join the 1867 union of Nova Scotia, New Brunswick, and present-day Ontario and Quebec, the initial conference was held in Charlottetown in 1864. Its rural beauty, historic atmosphere, fine sandy beaches, and renowned seafood, especially lobster, combine to make Prince Edward Island a popular destination for tourists.

Opposite: Grand Pré National Historic Park commemorates the poignant history of the French Acadians who settled this area of Nova Scotia.

Above: Fields near Park Corner, Prince Edward Island, display one of the island's most famous products—potatoes.

Opposite: Colourful clapboard buildings brighten Great George Street, in Charlottetown, the capital of Prince Edward Island.

Previous page: Snow emphasizes the charm of a brightly painted wooden home in Kings Landing, New Brunswick.

Above: Smoked herring at Seal Cove, on Grand Manan Island, New Brunswick.

Opposite: Halifax, the capital of Nova Scotia and an important seaport, is an intriguing mixture of old and new.

Previous page: Mist descends on the bright colours of fall in Nova Scotia's Annapolis Basin.

Above: Fishboats off Cape Sable Island, Nova Scotia; the area has a rich fishery and a long tradition of boat-building.

Opposite: The rocky shore of Prince Edward Island National Park, near Cavendish, displays the province's distinctive red soil.

Sawmill at Kings Landing Historical Settlement in New Brunswick, a 160-hectare outdoor museum containing more than seventy restored buildings.

Above: The waterfront at Charlottetown, Prince Edward Island's capital city.

Opposite: A traditional oxen pull attracts a crowd in Annapolis County, Nova Scotia.

Above: A winter scene on the Wheatley River, Prince Edward Island.

Opposite: The famous lighthouse at Peggy's Cove in Nova Scotia.

Quebec

The heart of French culture in Canada is found in Quebec, Canada's largest province. Its 6,896,000 people, who represent about 90 percent of Canada's French population, are concentrated to the south along the lowlands of the St. Lawrence River. The pleasant, fertile land of the St. Lawrence and the easy access it provided appealed to the first settlers, who parcelled the land into the long narrow sections fronting on the river that characterize the lowlands even today. Quebec's huge northern region is virtually uninhabited except for isolated settlements, many created as a result of industries such as mining and hydroelectric developments. Manufacturing, farming, forestry, hydroelectric power, and mining of gold, asbestos, and iron ore are the primary industries in Quebec.

Quebec City is known for the preservation of its historic areas.

Quebec's largest city, and the second largest in Canada, is Montreal, with a metropolitan population of 3,127,000. First a mission and later a centre for the fur trade, Montreal grew slowly. By the mid-1800s, it had taken its place as Canada's major financial and industrial centre, a position it retained until it was superceded by Toronto in the last few decades. Montreal's reputation as Canada's most sophisticated, cosmopolitan city remains secure, however. It is a fascinating mixture of French and English cultures, restored historic sites and modern architecture, a dynamic business core and neighbourly residential areas, beautiful parks and exciting night life. Mount Royal is one of the city's landmarks, the highest elevation in the city at 250 metres. Mount Royal Park offers outstanding views of the surrounding city, and in the winter, residents can skate and cross-country ski in

the heart of the city. A 30-metre-high cross at the summit commemorates the city's founding as a mission in 1643.

The capital of the province, Quebec City, is unique in North America. It is the seat of the only francophone administration on the continent and a city of great historic importance. Located at the narrowing of the St. Lawrence River, Quebec City was strategically important during the seventeenth and eighteenth centuries. Its role as the province's major metropolis was long ago usurped by Montreal, but Quebec City is still a major port and a magnet for tourists. Lower Town, by the St. Lawrence, and Upper Town, on the promontory above it, are the core of the old city, the only walled city in North America north of Mexico. The Citadel, built in 1820, historic buildings such as the Chateau Frontenac, and the narrow cobbled streets and stone buildings of the old residential area dating from the seventeenth and eighteenth centuries are remarkably well preserved. The area was designated a UN Heritage Site in 1985. Quebec's architecture and the lively street scene charm visitors, who can appreciate the city from horse-drawn carriages.

The St. Lawrence River is central to the identity of Quebec. For centuries it has been important to settlement, transportation, and industry, and about 90 percent of the province's population lives within a few kilometres of its banks. The St. Lawrence Lowlands area, the Appalachians to the south, and the Gaspé Peninsula are esteemed by Quebecers and visitors alike for recreational activities, such as skiing, camping, and general touring.

Opposite: The imposing Chateau Frontenac is the backdrop for a snowman during Quebec City's world-famous, eleven-day Winter Carnival.

Above: Sunset brings calm to the ocean at Carbes-Rosier, on the Gaspé Peninsula.

Opposite: The magnificent architecture of Notre Dame Cathedral, in Montreal.

Above: The Illuminated Crowd *in downtown Montreal, where modern office towers and public art contribute to the cosmopolitan atmosphere.*

Opposite: The limestone cliffs of Cap-Bon-Ami, in Forillon National Park, Quebec.

Previous page: An open-air sidewalk cafe contributes to a lively street scene.

Above: The brilliant fall colours for which Quebec is renowned, reflected in calm Lake Pohenagamook.

Opposite: The red sandstone cliffs of the Magdalen Islands, in the Gulf of St. Lawrence.

An aerial view captures the sparkle of Montreal by night.

The delicacy of flowers blowing in the wind is a counterpoint to the monolithic Percé Rock, a famous Gaspé Peninsula landmark.

A quiet corner in Gatineau Park, a region famous for spectacular fall colours.

Above: The shores of the Gaspé Peninsula are dotted with charming villages such as this.

Opposite: Viewers are dwarfed by the frozen cascade of Montmorency Falls, which plunges over an eighty-four-metre cliff.

Above: Ile du Cap aux Meules, one of the larger of the Magdalen Islands, boasts a coastline of rocky headlands and extensive sand dunes.

Opposite: The Chateau Frontenac in Quebec City, one of the CPR's famous string of chateau-style hotels built near the turn of the century.

Ontario

Canada's most populous and second-largest province, Ontario is also its most geologically diverse. Its northern edge borders the frigid salt water of Hudson Bay; to the south are the Great Lakes, with Canada's southernmost point, Point Pelee and its offshore islands. Ontario is sharply divided into northern and southern regions. Densely forested, rich in mineral wealth, criss-crossed by rivers and dotted with lakes, the north—90 percent of the land—is wilderness containing just 10 percent of the population. To the south are manufacturing centres and agricultural lands where most of the province's 10,085,000 people live. Fittingly, in a province where 16 percent of the area is covered by fresh water, Ontario's name comes from the Cree and means "beautiful water."

Ontario is also Canada's wealthiest province. Its agricultural land has been ranked the richest in Canada, and it possesses abundant hydroelectric resources. Other important aspects of the economy are forest-related industries, and mining of substantial deposits of nickel, copper, zinc, silver, gold, uranium, and iron ore. The north, a storehouse of mineral wealth, has more recently become recognized for its recreational potential. Ontario's central position in Canada, good energy supplies, and proximity to the United States have helped to make it Canada's leader in manufacturing, and it claims Canada's third-largest port—Thunder Bay, some 4,000 kilometres from the sea.

Toronto is the capital of Ontario and its largest city: approximately 3,893,000 people live within the metropolitan area. Once known as "Toronto the Good" for its somewhat dull and homogeneous Anglo-Saxon origins,

Summer visitors to Parliament Hill are treated to the stirring military ceremony of the Changing of the Guards.

it has emerged in the last few decades as a vibrant, cosmopolitan city with an exciting ethnocultural mix. A downtown core of modern skyscrapers centred on Bay Street attests to Toronto's position as the financial centre of Canada, but the city's architecture also reflects its historical roots. Buildings such as Casa Loma and Osgoode Hall, carefully restored historic homes like Campbell House and Gibson House, and traditional neighbourhood areas such as Kensington Market preserve important aspects of the city's heritage. Notable modern developments include the 40-hectare waterfront development and the CN Tower, the world's tallest free-standing structure at over 553 metres.

The city has spread and absorbed many smaller satellite communities, but outside its limits are the pretty towns and small vegetable, fruit, and tobacco farms that give this part of Ontario its rural charm.

Of course, no account of Ontario would be complete without including Niagara Falls. This stunning cascade, 675 metres wide and 54 metres high, has been attracting tourists since the early 1800s and still draws millions of visitors each year.

Ottawa, the capital city of Canada, is located on the south bank of the Ottawa River, across the river from its twin city, Hull, in Quebec. Ottawa-Hull is the fourth-largest urban centre in Canada, with a population of 921,000. A quiet sense of tradition pervades Ottawa, enhanced by the Parliament Buildings and other historic landmarks, the gracious residential areas, and many well-used parks and gardens. Parks and scenic driveways take advantage of Ottawa's outstanding natural location, preserving areas along the river and historic sites, such as the Rideau Canal.

Opposite: The Rideau Canal is used year-round by residents of Ottawa, who take full advantage of the pleasures that winter can bring.

Above: Old stone buildings on the main street of Unionville—an example of Ontario's historic heritage.

Opposite: Birch trees crackle with frost against a wintry blue sky.

Thousand Islands, an eighty-kilometre-long section of the St. Lawrence River, contains over one thousand rocky, wooded islands of varying sizes.

Ottawa is famed for its spring display of tulips, which commemorate Canada's aid to Holland during the Second World War.

The Toronto skyline and waterfront area have changed dramatically in the last few decades.

Above: A farmer and his dog stroll down a country road—a charming picture of rural Ontario.

Opposite: Upper Canada Village, a project developed in the 1950s and '60s, is a replica of a nineteenth-century St. Lawrence River community.

Above: Algonquin Provincial Park, established in 1893, contains numerous waterways and some 2,500 lakes.

Opposite: Toronto's office towers attest to the city's position as the financial centre of Canada.

Above: Toronto's multicultural mixture is celebrated in a wide array of festivals, including Caribana, a weekend extravaganza in August.

Opposite: The last rays of the sun illuminate the Toronto waterfront, dominated by the CN Tower and Skydome.

Above: Lake Ontario shoreline in the icy grip of winter.

Opposite: Aerial view of the stunning spectacle of 675-metre-wide Niagara Falls plunging over its 54-metre-high cliff.

Above: Toronto's Spadina and Dundas area has a rich ethnic mix, including Chinatown, which stretches along Dundas Street for several blocks.

Previous page: A crowd gathers at the Peace Tower on Parliament Hill for Canada Day celebrations.

At Upper Canada Village, guides in period costume explain and demonstrate the way of life of early inhabitants of Upper Canada.

Lake Superior, the largest freshwater lake in the world, in one of its calm moods.

Bales of hay in readiness for winter storage; Ontario's agricultural lands are considered to be the richest in Canada.

Above: The Ontario countryside is dotted with small churches, many built by the first settlers.

Opposite: Baling hay on an Ontario farm.

Ottawa's Canadian Museum of Civilization, housed in a spectacular building with a children's museum, traces the cultural heritage of Canada.

Early morning sun penetrates the mist at Algonquin Provincial Park.

Pukaskwa National Park, established in 1971, protects a rugged wilderness of rocky shorelines, turbulent rivers, and abundant wildlife.

Since 1830, farmers have been selling their produce at Ottawa's Byward Market.

Above: The rugged landscape near Thunder Bay is typical of the Canadian Shield, which stretches to the shores of Lake Superior.

Opposite: Commuters stream homeward on a Toronto freeway.

Manitoba

Manitoba is considered to be one of the three prairie provinces, but it is also a place of transition—between east and west, and between the rocky, treed terrain of the Precambrian Shield and the agricultural lands of the prairies. The southwestern portion of the province, about one-third of its total area, is a fertile plain that supports the province's agricultural industry. Most of Manitoba's population is concentrated here.

Winnipeg is the capital and largest city, with a population of 652,000, well over half the province's total of 1,091,000. Established at the confluence of the Red and Assiniboine rivers, Winnipeg became a boom town in its early years, when the completion of the CPR gave the city strategic importance. Situated at the geographic centre of Canada, it maintains an important position as an essential transportation link today. Several turn-of-the-century highrises remain on its main street, somewhat dwarfed by the skyscrapers of the modern city but an important part of the city landscape. Another architectural landmark is the Legislative Building. Built of Manitoba's Tindall limestone, the Legislature is topped with the four-metre-high "Golden Boy," sheathed in gold and holding a torch aloft.

Winnipeg has gained a reputation as a major cultural centre. It is the home of the renowned Royal Winnipeg Ballet, the Winnipeg Symphony Orchestra, an active theatre community, and numerous museums and art galleries. The annual Manitoba Music Festival is the largest in Canada. Folklorama, a week-long festival established in 1970, and individual festivals celebrate the

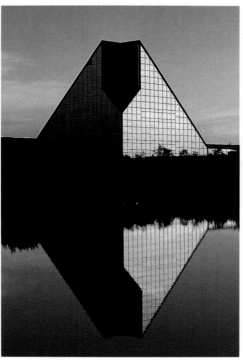

Sunset gilds the Royal Canadian Mint in Winnipeg.

ethnic diversity that is part of Winnipeg's lively character.

North of the city, Lake Winnipeg is a popular recreational area. One of the favourite destinations is the long, pure white, sandy beaches and eight-metre-high dunes of Grand Beach Provincial Park. Spanning the transition between east and west, Lake Winnipeg's eastern shore shows the rugged edge of the Canadian Shield in granite outcroppings; the marshy margins of the western shore are habitat for many bird species. Lakes Winnipeg, Winnipegosis and Manitoba are vestiges of what was once the world's largest freshwater lake. Lake Agassiz covered most of southern Manitoba; its retreat, about 8,000 years ago after the last Ice Age, left a thick deposit of silt that is the basis of Manitoba's fertile farmlands. Agriculture still plays a prominent role in the economy, along with manufacturing, mining, and production of hydroelectricity.

The vast hinterland of the north is dotted with countless smaller lakes and rivers. Manitoba is able to supply its own hydroelectric power needs and exports to other provinces. A mecca for wilderness enthusiasts, Manitoba's remote northern fishing and hunting camps are increasingly popular with residents and visitors to the province.

Manitoba's northernmost centre is Churchill, on Hudson Bay. Canada's only seaport on the Arctic, Churchill's port is open for navigation just three months of the year. The town's attractions include the opportunity to see polar bears, beluga whales, and rare bird species in the wild.

Opposite: Verdant fields contrast with the "big sky" of the prairies.

Glorious sunset colours reflect in Clear Lake, in Riding Mountain National Park.

Cemetery at St. Boniface Cathedral, the burial site of Metis leader Louis Riel.

Above: Prairie roads, such as this near Ste. Agathe, divide the fertile farmlands into precise geometric divisions.

Opposite: A wind-blown flax field in blossom, near Dufresne.

Previous page: The Forks, a redevelopment project in the centre of Winnipeg, brings together recreational, cultural, and commercial activities at an historic meeting place.

Opposite: View from Baldy Mountain, in Duck Mountain Provincial Park.

Below: Ice floes on the banks of the Churchill River near Churchill.

Above: Portage and Main, the heart of Winnipeg's downtown area.

Opposite: Sheathed in gold, the four-metre-high Golden Boy crowning Manitoba's Legislative Building holds aloft a torch; it was electrically lit in 1970, the province's centenary.

Saskatchewan

Carved with geometric precision from the middle of the great plains, the image most often associated with Saskatchewan is the flat tablelands of the southern agricultural half of the province. As far as the eye can see, fields lie flat under the prairie sky, a landscape broken only by the squared-off symmetry of roads, occasional stands of deciduous trees, farms, and small towns where the most outstanding landmark is the ever-present grain elevator.

Saskatchewan's two largest cities, representing close to half the province's population of 989,000, are in this sector of the province. The provincial capital, Regina, has created its own oasis in the dry plains with Wascana Centre, a 920-hectare area surrounding man-made Wascana Lake. The Legislative Buildings, University of Regina, and Saskatchewan Centre of the Arts are all located here. As well as being the seat of government, Regina is the corporate centre of the province and the site of the RCMP's only training facilities since 1985. The RCMP Centennial Museum commemorates the Mounties' history here. Just north of Regina, the Qu'Appelle Valley carves a verdant path through the prairies. The rolling hills of the valley surround the river and a string of eight lakes that stretch from Buffalo Pound in the west to Round Lake in the east, a welcome respite from the harsh southern landscape.

Saskatoon, the province's largest city at 210,000 and a lively artistic community, is prettily situated on the South Saskatchewan River. The city has grown up on both sides of the river, which is spanned by seven bridges. The venerable Bessborough Hotel and a number of churches

Wheatfield in the Qu'Appelle Valley.

are landmarks on the west bank, where riverside parks take advantage of the setting. Opposite is the University of Saskatchewan campus with its attractive greystone buildings.

Saskatoon is a hub for the central and northern area of the province, where both agriculture and resource development play a role. Primarily an agricultural province, Saskatchewan is one of the largest producers of wheat in the world, and the largest in Canada by a generous margin. Other important agricultural products are canola, rye, oats, barley, and flax. Petroleum, natural gas, uranium, and especially potash play a part in the provincial economy.

Montreal Lake, near Prince Albert National Park, is the geographic centre of the province, a transitional region between the settled, dry agricultural belt of the south and the largely uninhabited northern reaches. Thousands of lakes and rivers irrigate huge tracts of wilderness—surprisingly, in a province that most people associate with dry conditions, 12 percent of Saskatchewan's area is fresh water. Guided hunting and fishing tours, and whitewater rafting expeditions on one of the country's great rivers, the Churchill, contribute to the province's growing tourism industry.

Far to the south are more surprising aspects of this prairie province. The Cypress Hills jut abruptly from the prairie in the southwest, the rolling slopes fed by numerous springs that rise in the hills. This corner of the prairies escaped the great ice sheets, and there are many species of plant and animal that are found in the Rocky Mountains, over 200 kilometres to the west.

Opposite: Saskatchewan's Legislative Building, on Wascana Lake in Regina.

Regina has been the headquarters for basic training of RCMP constables since 1886.

Echo Lake, in Echo Valley Provincial Park, in the scenic Qu'Appelle Valley.

Above: Cypress Hills Provincial Park is a unique region of rolling hills, stands of lodgepole pine, wildflowers, and native animals.

Opposite: Saskatoon's venerable Bessborough Hotel is a landmark on the west bank of the Saskatchewan River.

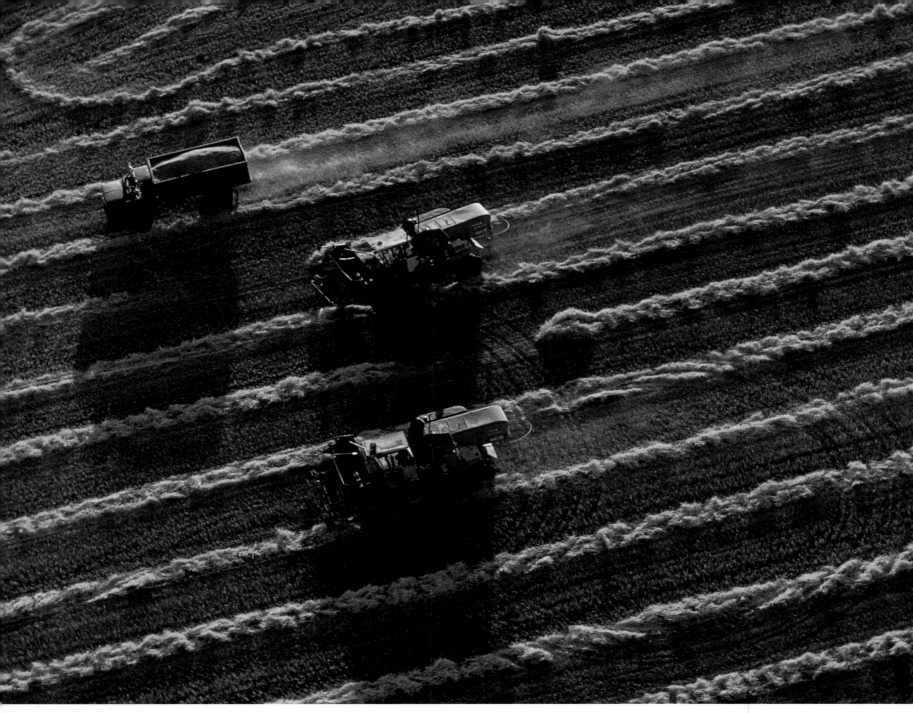

Above: An aerial view reveals the precise patterns of harvesting.

Previous page: Grain elevators, like these at Webb, stand like sentinels at every prairie town.

Batoche National Historic Site preserves the remains of the Metis village of Batoche, including St. Antoine de Padoue church and rectory.

Alberta

Prairie sunsets, cowboys riding the range, open plains as far as the eye can see, and world-renowned mountain parks: Alberta contains within its borders some of the most dramatic landscapes in Canada.

Alberta's capital and largest city, Edmonton is Canada's most northerly major metropolis. Begun as an outpost of the Hudson's Bay Company in the late 1700s, Edmonton didn't come to prominence until a century and a half later, with the 1947 discovery of oil at Leduc. Today it is a thriving city with a population of 840,000, an agricultural centre and a transportation hub for the riches of the remote north. A sign of its status is the West Edmonton Mall, which covers 45 hectares and contains hundreds of shops and services and a variety of amenities, including two indoor lakes, an eighteen-hole miniature golf course, and the world's largest indoor amusement park.

The foothills and south-central area is prime grazing land, where large cattle spreads still operate. Calgary, a close second to Edmonton in population at 754,000, is the gateway to the Rockies and the supply centre for the south. Located on the Bow River, Calgary has grown from the "Sandstone City"—its old City Hall, the Alberta Hotel, and other buildings date from this period when the public buildings were all constructed of local sandstone—to a modern city of skyscrapers housing corporate headquarters. Even with its new oil-based affluence, the city remembers its ranching heritage. The Calgary Stampede, a ten-day rodeo extravaganza in July,

The impressive skyline of Calgary, Alberta's second-largest city.

attracts visitors from around the world.

Alberta has preserved much of its Rocky Mountain area in national and provincial parks and reserves. The best-known of these is Banff National Park. Created in 1887, Banff was Canada's first national park and remains one of the country's premier attractions today. At 6,640 square kilometres, Banff National Park has something for everyone. Its slopes offer some of the best skiing in the world. Within the village of Banff is the Banff Centre for the Arts, the luxurious Banff Springs Hotel, and a variety of services. Much-photographed Lake Louise, with its elegant Chateau, never seems to lose its appeal. And the natural beauty and abundant wildlife that first impressed its founders is still one of the foremost attractions of the park today. More than 1,500 kilometres of trails allow access to pristine wilderness areas. To the north is Jasper National Park, and connecting Banff and Jasper townsites is the Icefields Parkway. One of the great highways of the world, it offers unparalleled views of glaciers, towering peaks, crevasses, canyons, mountain rivers, and waterfalls.

To the south, Waterton National Park adjoins Montana's Glacier National Park, the world's first international peace park. Here the mountains rise abruptly from the prairies and the park encompasses a wide range of habitats. Alberta's famed badlands, one of the world's richest repositories of ancient fossils, centre around the Red Deer River Valley in eastern Alberta. A wind-carved landscape of hoodoos and gullies with its own eerie beauty, Dinosaur Provincial Park is a UN World Heritage Site.

Opposite: Paddlers on Moraine Lake, in Banff National Park.

Above: A peaceful scene on Herbert Lake, in Banff National Park.

Opposite: Fall colour near Columbia Icefields in Banff National Park.

Previous page: The Edmonton skyline, dwarfed by the prairie sky.

Above: The cool light of a winter morning illuminates granaries near Leduc at dawn.

Opposite: The Rockies form a breathtaking backdrop to a farm near Longview.

Above: A stormy sky presages more snow for the Fairholme Range.

Previous page: Maligne Lake, in Jasper National Park, is the largest lake in the Rockies.

110

A prairie road beckons travellers to distant mountains.

Above: Wranglers in Willmore Wilderness Provincial Park, north of Jasper.

Opposite: Barn and rangeland near Payne Lake, Alberta.

113

The West Edmonton Mall is the largest shopping centre in the world, with more than eight hundred stores and services, pools, ice rinks, a water park, and numerous other attractions.

Built in 1875, the McDougall Church, near Cochrane, was the first church in Canada for native people.

Above: At Athabasca Falls, in Jasper National Park, the river takes a twelve-metre plunge through a narrow gorge.

Opposite: Grain elevators at Standard.

Previous page: The glacial waters of Peyto Lake, in Banff National Park.

Above: Abundant wildlife, such as this mountain goat, roams the Rocky Mountains.

Opposite: Alberta's badlands are a region of deep gullies and hoodoos, sculpted over time by the forces of erosion.

The Banff Springs Hotel, set in one of the most majestic natural settings in the world, still maintains a reputation for luxury established at the turn of the century.

The Icefields Parkway, which connects Banff and Jasper townsites, traverses some of the most stupendous mountain scenery in the world.

Bull riding is one of the toughest events at the world-famous Calgary Stampede.

Above: Jasper townsite, in Jasper National Park.

Opposite: The calm waters of Beauvert Lake in Jasper National Park reflect a muted sunset.

Above: Cowboys at work in Alberta's cattle country.

Opposite: Fairview Mountain, 2,774 metres, appears to rise straight from the turquoise waters of Banff's Lake Louise.

Moraine Lake, in Banff, is a popular destination for hikers and paddlers.

Summer fallow and a new crop at Drumheller.

Above: Banff is world-famous for its winter ski facilities, but everyday pursuits are also enjoyed in this magnificent mountain setting.

Opposite: Alpine meadows burst into bloom in the Valley of the Ten Peaks, Banff National Park.

British Columbia

Canada's Pacific province is inevitably associated with the sea. Its coastline, almost 26,000 kilometres long, is an intricate maze of islands and inlets, where a mild climate and abundant rainfall encourage the exuberant growth of Canada's temperate rainforest. The coast is both a huge recreational playground and a working ocean. British Columbia's ports, with their proximity to expanding Asian markets, are some of the fastest-growing in Canada. Huge runs of salmon spawn in the coastal rivers, attracting both commercial fleets and recreational anglers throughout the season. Sailors choose among countless uninhabited coves, busy metropolitan ports, or marinas on picturesque populated islands up and down the coast. With the increasing interest in wildlife, whale-watching tours are a fast-growing industry.

Hiking in the lush rainforest at Naikoon Provincial Park in the Queen Charlotte Islands.

Yet the coast is just one aspect of this diverse province. From salt water to the border with Alberta, a series of mountain ranges, fertile valleys, and plateaus dominate the landscape. The hot dry summers and expansive irrigation systems produce the abundant fruit and grape crops of the interior valleys. On the rolling hills of the dry interior plateau, the huge ranch spreads of the Cariboo-Chilcotin recall a way of life of a century ago. Sparsely settled, this area combines the romance of the cowboy with the lively history of the Cariboo Gold Rush of the 1860s. Farther north is the wheat-growing area of the Peace River and the myriad lakes of the far north, as yet little disturbed by the inroads of human settlement. Mining and forestry are major industries, but tourism is also staking a claim in the backcountry, with camping, skiing, and guided wilderness tours.

Moderated by the warm ocean current, British Columbia boasts the balmiest temperatures in Canada. When much of the country suffers through temperatures well below freezing, coastal British Columbia often basks in warm breezes and sunshine. The capital city, Victoria, enjoys the most temperate weather in the province. Occupying the southernmost tip of Vancouver Island, its lovely setting is enhanced by extravagant parks and gardens, public and private. A relatively small city with a population of 287,897, Victoria has an old-time ambience. A gracious residential area surrounds the downtown core centred on the harbour. The Legislative Buildings and the venerable Empress Hotel are central to a commercial area marked by turn-of-the-century architecture and sympathetically designed modern buildings. The British Columbia Museum is a tour-de-force of interactive displays that tell the story of British Columbia from its first peoples through later settlement.

Vancouver is British Columbia's largest city, and Canada's third largest, with a metropolitan population of 1,602,000. Its surroundings are impressive: cradled between the mountains and the sea, and spreading out through the wide and fertile Fraser Valley and its delta, Vancouver residents boast that they can golf or sail in the morning and ski in the afternoon. In the last decades of this century, Vancouver has undergone a transformation. From a sleepy backwater, somewhat mockingly known as "Lotusland," it has taken its place on the world stage as a sophisticated city, commercial hub of the province, and gateway to the countries of the Pacific Rim.

Opposite: A bird's-eye view of Burrard Bridge, Granville Island, downtown Vancouver, and the North Shore mountains.

Dry hills near Ashcroft, a near-desert area where cattle range over rolling hills covered in sagebrush, cactus, and tumbleweed.

Butchart Gardens, north of Victoria, were begun in an abandoned limestone quarry and have grown into a world-renowned, twenty-hectare public garden.

Above: Cyclists pause to appreciate the spring display of cherry blossoms in Stanley Park, Vancouver.

Opposite: The Gulf Islands are a sailor's paradise, offering a myriad of protected coves among pristine coastal scenery.

Above: Rugged ranchland in the dry country near Lillooet in the south Cariboo.

Opposite: The ten-kilometre seawall along the perimeter of Stanley Park affords panoramic views of Vancouver's harbour, the North Shore, and on a clear day, the mountains of Vancouver Island.

A harvest moon adds a touch of magic to this night-time view of Vancouver and the Lions Gate Bridge.

Cattle graze in a narrow valley near Jaffray, in British Columbia's Rocky Mountains.

The Sealink, a passenger-only ferry to Victoria and Nanaimo, speeds away from its Vancouver dock at Canada Place.

Above: Detail of totem pole in Stanley Park.

Opposite: Spring display of tulips at Fantasy Gardens, one of Vancouver's many public gardens.

Above: On Vancouver Island's west coast, the strength of the stormy Pacific can be felt even in Tofino's protected harbour.

Previous page: The moon rises over a pristine lake in Garibaldi Provincial Park.

The Museum of Anthropology at the University of British Columbia is an important storehouse of the art and culture of the province's First Nations people.

Above: The Empress Hotel presides over Victoria's harbour.

Previous page: As the sun sets, fog begins to settle over the waters of Barkley Sound, on the west coast of Vancouver Island.

Mixed forest and grasslands cover the rolling uplands near Kamloops.

Fruit trees in bloom in the sunny Okanagan Valley, an important fruit-growing region.

The west coast of Vancouver Island is a lush mix of rocky, wave-battered headlands, lush coastal forest, and long, sandy beaches.

A hiker surveys a receding vista of mountain peaks from the top of Idaho Peak.

British Columbia's Legislative Buildings, just above Victoria's harbour, were built in 1897.

Dawn breaks over Citadel Pass in Mount Assiniboine Provincial Park.

A view of the ocean from the West Coast Trail, a rugged, several-day hike between Bamfield and Port Renfrew on Vancouver Island.

The Northwest Territories and the Yukon

Canada's far north, an immense region encompassing almost 40 percent of the country's total area, excites varying responses. To some, it is a land of incomparable beauty, a pristine wilderness where humans are happily forced to concede the superior power of nature. United for survival, the bonds between people are strong. To others, it is an unforgiving land where darkness reigns for many months and temperatures rarely rise above freezing. But most of those who come in contact with the north concede that it possesses a powerful mystique.

The warm glow of a camp tent is welcome as dusk gathers on the Porcupine River in the Yukon.

The Northwest Territories extends from Baffin Island in the east to the Yukon in the west and includes a great number of islands in the Arctic Archipelago. Its 58,000 people—of whom about 51 percent are first nations, Inuit and Dene—are spread thinly over 3.4 million square kilometres. Yellowknife, on the north arm of Great Slave Lake, is its capital and the only city, with some 15,000 people. Originally the site of a fur-trading post, Yellowknife enjoyed a boom period during the thirties when gold was discovered. Today it is a mining centre and headquarters for tours to more remote parts of the Northwest Territories. The city is a contrast of new and old, with the brightly coloured buildings of the Dene village, artifacts from the early gold-mining days, and some of the most up-to-date facilities in the north. Wood Buffalo National Park, south of Great Slave Lake, is one of three national parks in the Northwest Territories, including Auyuittuq, on the east coast of Baffin Island. Nahanni, in the Mackenzie Mountains to the west, is a

paradise for wilderness adventurers, with whitewater rivers, craggy mountains, and abundant wildlife. It was declared a UN World Heritage Site in 1979.

Like the Northwest Territories, the Yukon's economy relies heavily on mining. The storied Klondike Gold Rush of 1896-1904 was the first major mining venture here, but now other ores, such as zinc, lead, and copper, are also mined. At the peak of the gold rush, Dawson's population was estimated at 40,000. Today there are less than a thousand residents, but this number swells each summer when tourists come to relive the lively days of the gold rush. Whitehorse, named the capital in 1953, is the Yukon's largest urban centre, with 18,000 of the territory's 28,000 people. Located on the Yukon River, the city has become a major centre for the expanding tourism industry.

The haunting beauty of the Yukon draws hundreds of thousands of visitors annually. They trek north, some following in the footsteps of the goldseekers, others seeking the profound sense of wilderness to be found here. The St. Elias Range in Kluane National Park boasts Canada's highest mountain, Mount Logan, at 5,950 metres. The park encompasses some of the most breathtaking scenery in the world: uncharted peaks, the largest concentration of glaciers and ice fields in the world, wild and beautiful rivers, and a wide variety of wildlife. Some 250 kilometres of trails allow exploration of Kluane, which was named a UN World Heritage Site in 1979 for its untouched beauty and unique combinations of wildlife.

Opposite: Kayakers travel in traditional fashion in the frigid waters of north Baffin Island, in the Northwest Territories.

Above: Robert Service, here played by an actor, immortalized the territory in his poetry; today his cabin is part of Dawson's historic ambience.

Opposite: Horses graze in the Yukon's Ogilvie Mountains.

166

Above: Canoeing in the Northwest Territories.

Opposite: Inuit woman and child at Igloolik, in the Northwest Territories.

Previous page: Grise Fiord on Ellesmere Island, Canada's northernmost town, appears tenuous and fragile when set against the vastness of this northern land.

Above: The brief northern summer frees the land from the fierce grip of ice and snow.

Opposite: Miles Canyon on the Yukon River, once a barrier to Klondike prospectors, has been tamed by hydroelectric development.

Above: View from the Dempster Highway, which links the Yukon and Northwest Territories, crossing some of the most beautiful and isolated terrain in Canada.

Opposite: Dawson's summer celebration of the Klondike gold rush draws thousands of visitors to the Gaslight Follies each year.

Previous page: Whitewater rafters take on the rapids of the Firth River in the Yukon.

A group of hikers challenges winter conditions at Frobisher Bay on Baffin Island in the Northwest Territories.

The bright colours of fall presage the long, dark days of the northern winter.

Previous page: A wintry scene near Beaver Creek on the Alaska Highway.

183

Photo Credits

Craig Aurness/*First Light*
p. 98

Rose Blanche/*First Light*
p. 2

Michael E. Burch
pp. 110, 111, 115, 116-117, 120, 122-123, 124-125, 127, 128, 130, 138, 147, 156, 157

J. Cochrane/*First Light*
p. 48

Gera Dillon/*First Light*
p. 38

Dawn Goss/*First Light*
pp. 102-103, 105

Chris Harris/*First Light*
pp. 119, 132, 140

Richard Hartmier/*First Light*
pp. 68, 144-145, 154-155, 160-161, 166, 177, 180-181, 182-18

Stephen Homer/*First Light*
pp. 21, 39, 46

Thomas Kitchin/*First Light*
pp. 13, 16, 20, 28, 36, 37, 42, 45, 52, 63, 74, 91, 93, 96-97, 100, 104, 106, 133, 142, 158

Jerry Kobalenko/*First Light*
pp. 7, 168-169, 178-179

Todd Korol/*First Light*
p. 95

Robert Lankinen/*First Light*
p. 76

Scott Leslie/*First Light*
pp. 18-19

Larry MacDougal/*First Light*
p. 126